The Beginner's Guide to Australian Aboriginal Art

The symbols, their meanings and some Dreamtime stories.

Contents

Introduction

Written language can be loosely said to fall into two categories: the ancient hieroglyphic (pictorial) variety and the more recent alphabetic type. The former allows for the use of the imagination in reading; as often as not the meaning of a glyph can change relative to the group with which it appears. This system also lends itself to punning. For example the Egyptian hieroglyphs for the Goddess Isis were:

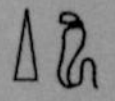

but Isis was also the star Sirius. These symbols can likewise be read as 'the rising of Serpent's tooth'. The serpent is universally associated with wisdom, and teeth represented stones which were, throughout the ancient world, symbolic of stars. Thus the glyphs not only represent the name 'Isis', but indicate a rising star. Further, Isis means 'seat of stone' or 'star womb'; she gave birth to the children of the stars, the magi. We might think of this system as intuitive, creative, feminine—Lunar. The modern alphabet is pedantic in the extreme: a D.O.G. is nothing other than a dog and a C.A.T. is an equally unequivocal cat. This form of written communication might be described as literal, scientific, masculine—Solar.

The Hebrew/Aramaic of the Old Testament of the Bible represents a transition from one form to the other. For example, one of the names of the biblical creator in whose image we are said to be made is Yahweh/Jehovah. In the original, which reads from right to left, his name is spelt with the letters: *yod,he,vau,he*, יהוה. If we set these down vertically 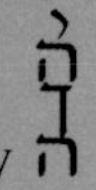 , we have a picture of the image in which we are made. The name Joshua (Jesus) is spelt exactly as Jehovah but with the letter *shin* in the middle, יהושה. The word *shin* means 'tooth', or 'stone', and Jesus terms himself 'the stone which the builders rejected'.

Where modern man is constantly looking at the ground to see what he might find, that he might profit from it, ancient man was constantly gazing at the stars in which he might see the future and become a prophet. But his knowledge was esoteric and, accordingly, his system of writing was designed to speak to a chosen initiated few. But then, what modern man finds on the ground he, like a dog with a bone, buries in a bank and will not share with any one at all.

Curiously, the ancient magician or shaman (the Aboriginal *wirinun*) invariably gave his *gnosis* (spiritual knowledge) the feminine gender, and the Bible always complies with this. The letter *teth*—the origin of teeth—means ‘snake’, and universally, esoteric wisdom is represented by the snake which, more often than not, is a female symbol. Interestingly enough, if we write the English ‘he’ (a male) and then precede this with the serpent-like ‘s’, we have ‘she’. Is it then indeed true that when God made man she was only joking?

Ancient myth, no matter where it originates, commonly speaks of a magic tree and a great flood, and relates the marriage of Father Sky and Mother Earth, who together produce the twelve tribes of humanity, which later become the children of the stars or twelve heavenly wanderers—the zodiac.

One form in which these appear is a pyramid-like mountain of stones which makes up a holy temple, or zigurat. Accordingly, because ancient astronomy was concerned with the precession of the equinoxes and the division of time by twelve (solar) or thirteen (lunar) segments, there are common but guarded references to a stone which the temple builders rejected.

Furthermore, because our bodies are largely water and because this falls from Father Sky and fertilizes the earth, this element was spoken of as the creator’s *sperma*. And then, because the true children of God were adepts in the ‘knowledge’ of the stars, water was often used as a symbol for divine *gnosis*. These magi were then said to walk on water (stand upon God’s word) or emerge from the sea (the watery womb of the earth) as fish or part fish/part man—God’s sperm-like fishes. The Aborigines of Australia were once party to this way of thinking. For example, the Aboriginal symbol for woman (see page 3) is an inverted horseshoe, and this precise symbol was used by the ancient Egyptians to write the number ten. This 1 and 0 is invariably representative of unity. And then there are the Aboriginal Three Sisters (see page 8) who came down from the stars of Orion’s Belt. In Egypt there was a triple-headed Goddess, and like so many other peoples, the Egyptians believed that life on earth originated from the stars of Orion.

Sadly, like all the related systems around the globe, that of the Aborigines too is now in a considerable state of disrepair—but it can, with patience, be retrieved.

So saying, let me take you gently by the pages and lead you on an exciting quest for the Holy Grail of the Dreamtime.

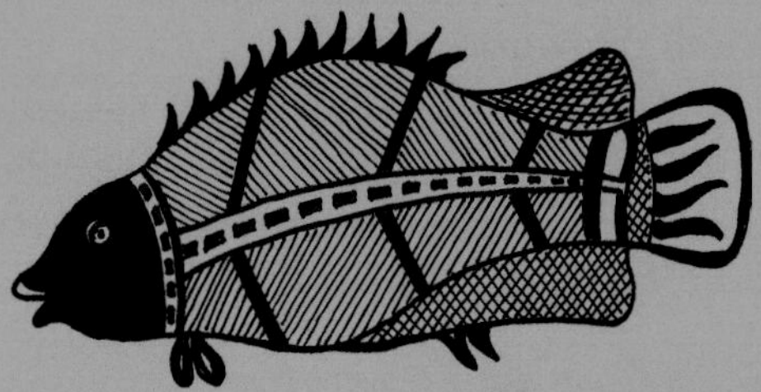

Part One *- Aboriginal symbols and their meanings*

I shall never forget my first encounter with Aboriginal Art. The man told me he had a painting he wanted to sell. Then as he began to unroll it, he said: ‘But it’s not a painting, it’s a story’. What my European eyes encountered was a great jumble of dots and symbols, which formed themselves into patterns. Slowly, as this fellow began to explain the meaning of the glyphs, a wonderful tale began to unravel. At that moment, this prince among story-tellers opened for me a door to a whole new world of sunshine and mystery, romance and adventure—the landscape of the never-ending story.

man

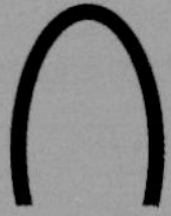

woman

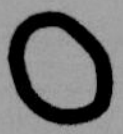

child

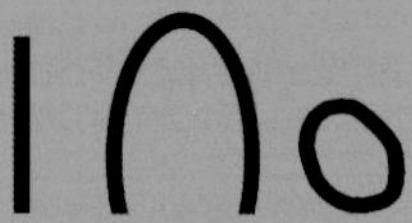

family

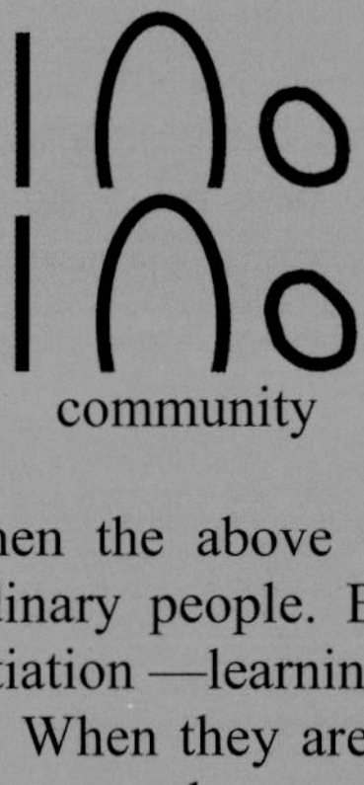

community

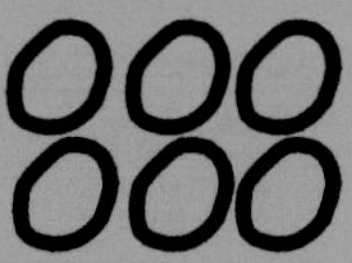

tribes

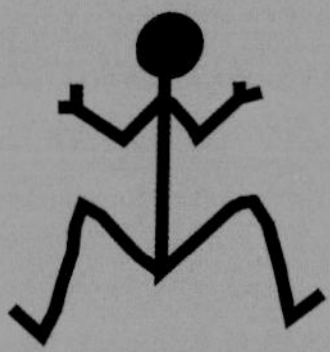

spirit ancestor

When the above symbols appear in dark colours, and as shown, they are ordinary people. But when surrounded by dots 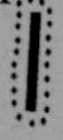 they are in process of initiation —learning the Dreaming.

When they are white, they are fully initiated *wirinuns* (shamans). In this instance, the sequence—egg, horseshoe and stick—indicates degrees of initiation, to the point of being able to live in two worlds—that of the body and that of the spirit. Indeed, they had the ability to speak with spirit ancestors, to live in both the world of the one and the zero. For this reason it was as common to find an initiated woman as to encounter an initiated man. Notably, this symbol is precisely the same as the Egyptian hieroglyph for the number fifty. This ‘fifty’ was the Nun into which Atum ejaculated the universe.

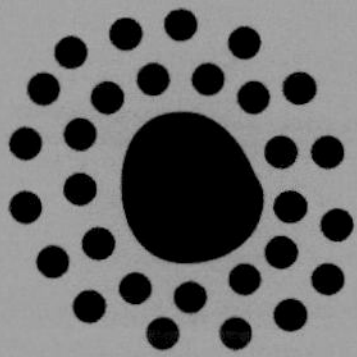

Emu
(Earth Mother)

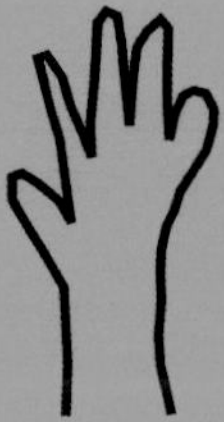

Sun
(Father of Destiny)

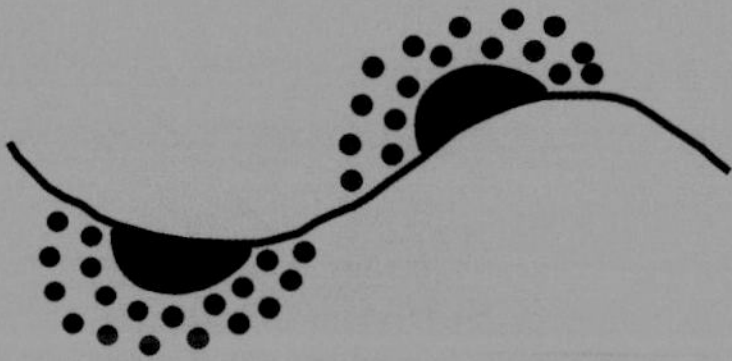

Dreaming track with
Emu/Earth Mother
energy rising from it

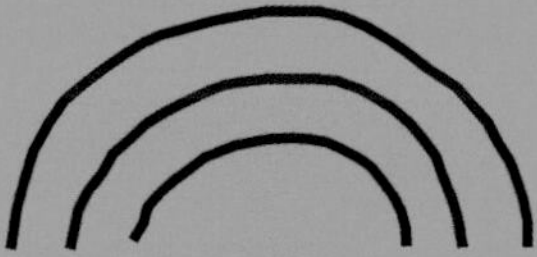

Rainbow

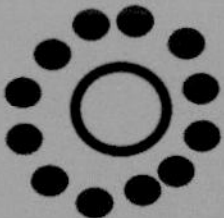

star

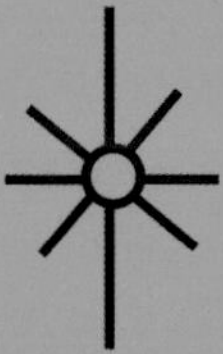

Venus

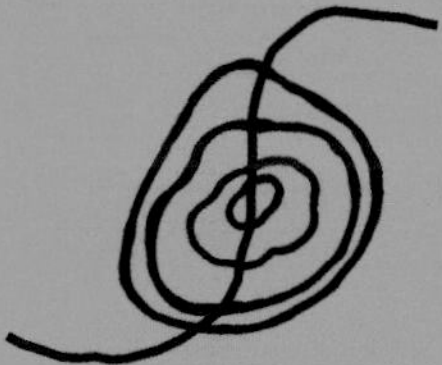

hill or
holy mound

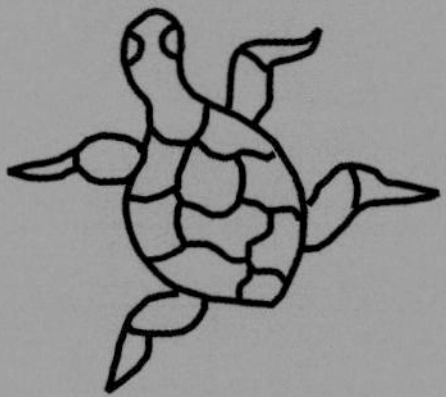

Scorpio (Turtle)

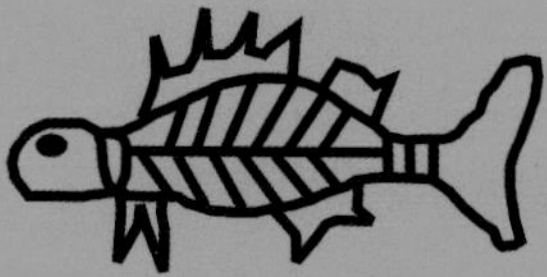

Pisces

cave

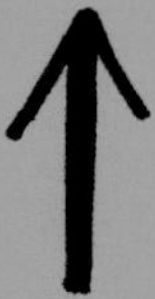

Tracks

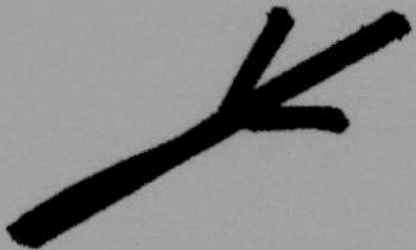

emu tracks

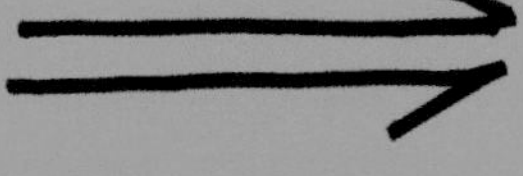

kangaroo tracks

or

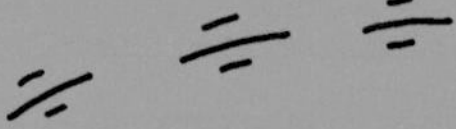

kangaroo tracks

or

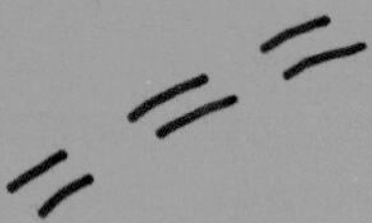

kangaroo tracks

hunter

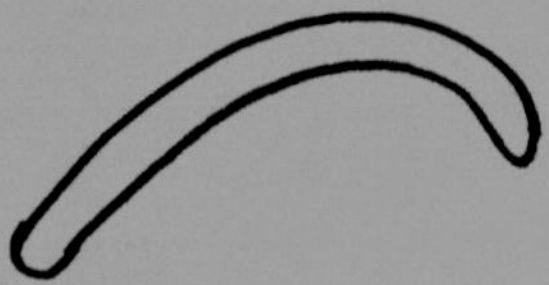

hunting/going hunting

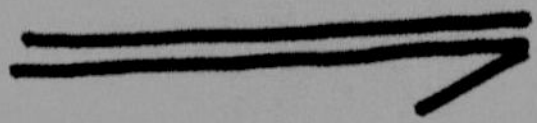

spear

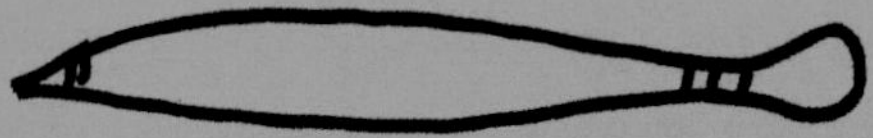

spear thrower

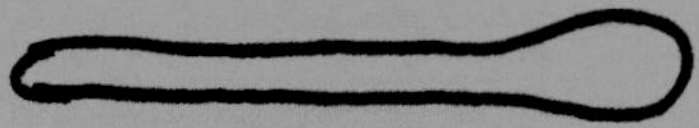

club (nulla nulla)

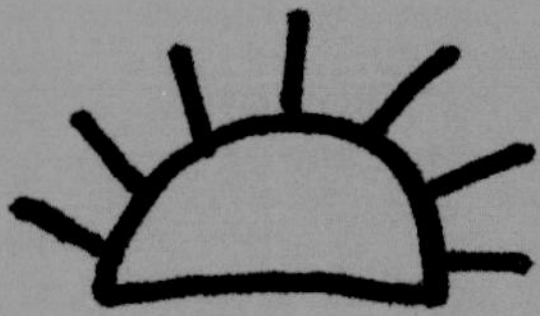

possum tracks

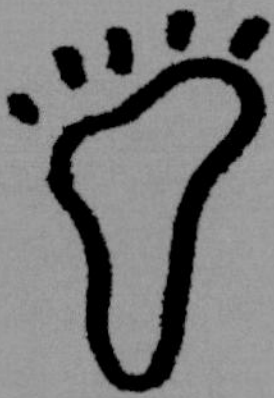

human tracks

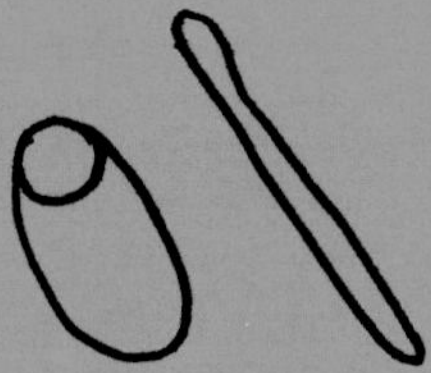

coolaman (dish)
and digging stick

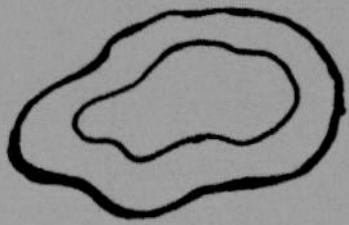

soak hole

rock hole

resting place

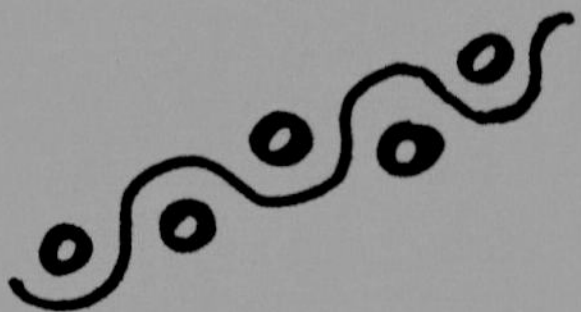

goanna tracks

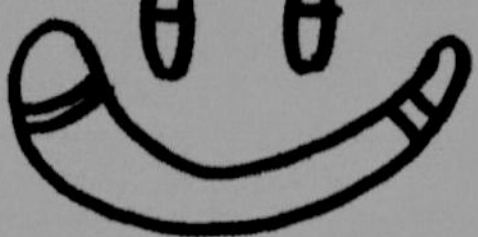

dingo tracks

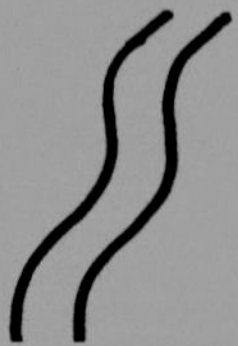

creek bed

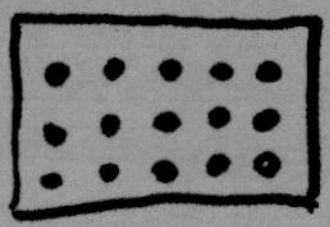
lightning

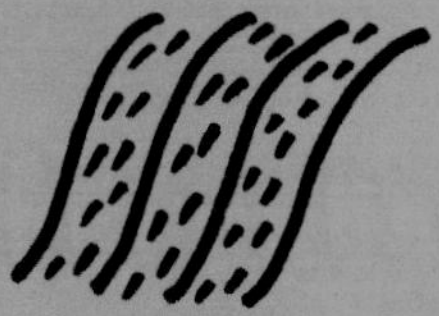
rain

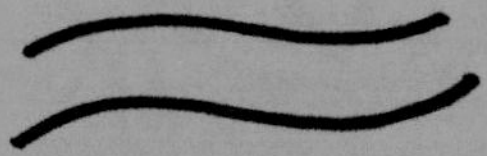
clouds

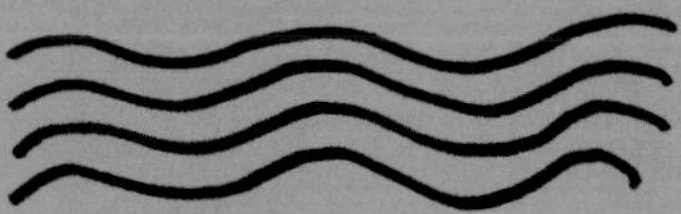
water/blood
(genealogy/descent)

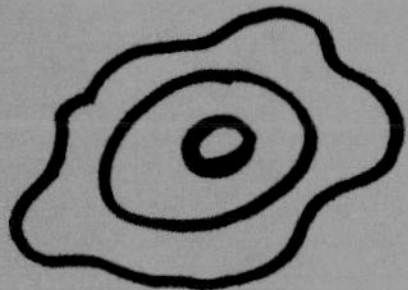
waterhole

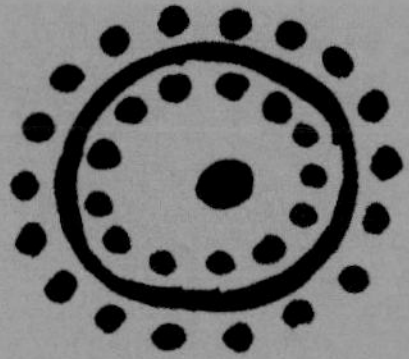
campsite

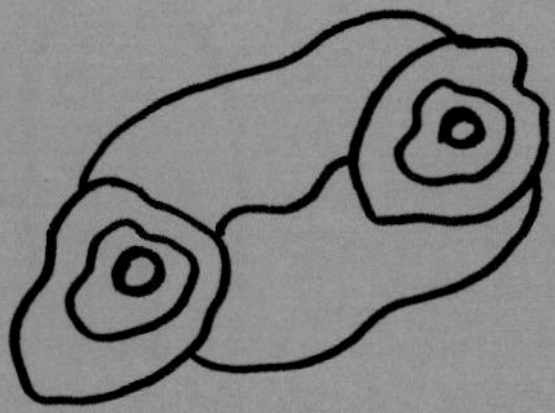
waterhole with
running water

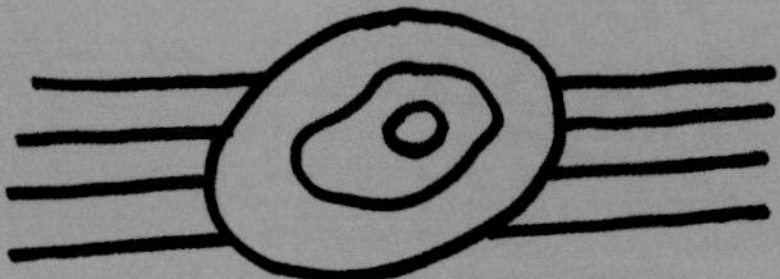
resting place with
running water

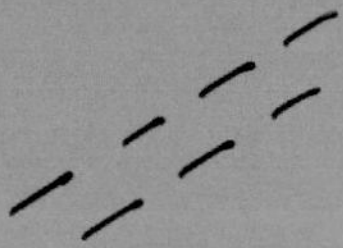
human tracks

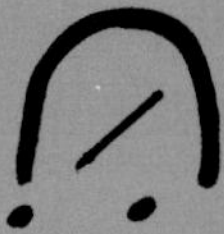
camp with fire

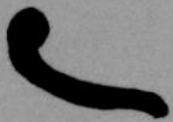
sleeping person

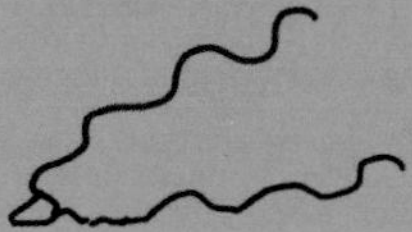
two snakes
entering hole

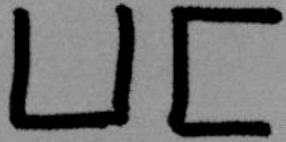
people sitting

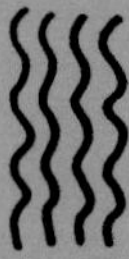
smoke

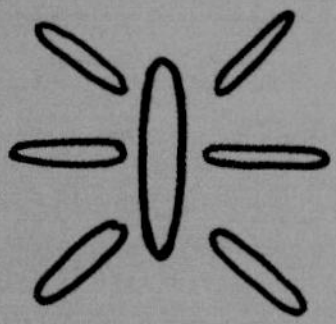
campfire

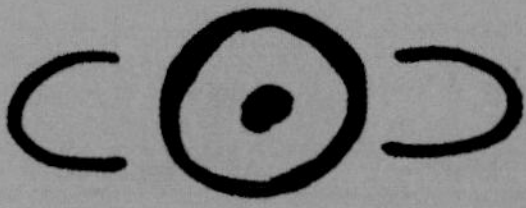
women cooking

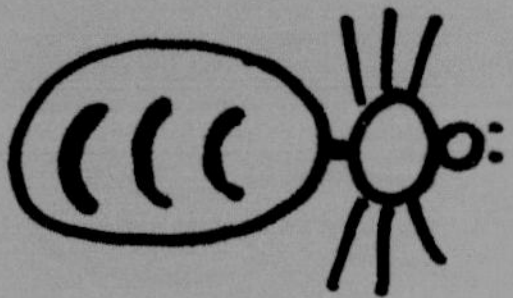

honey ants

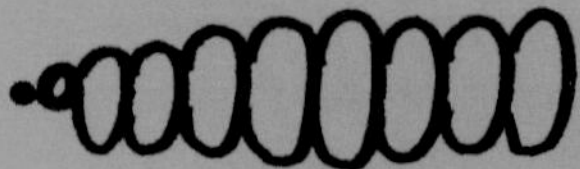

witchetty grubs

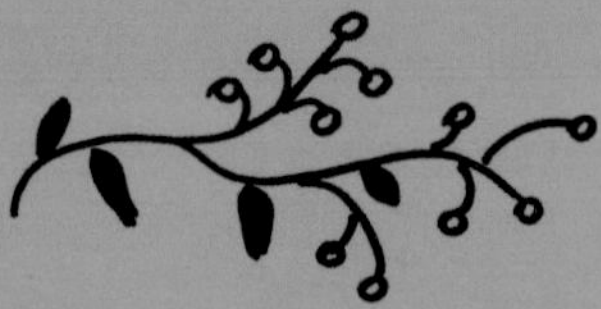

bush raisins

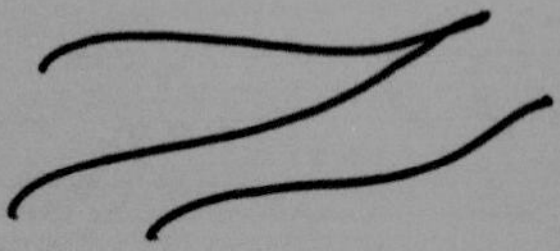

creek

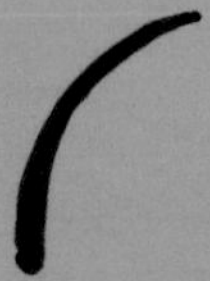

wind break

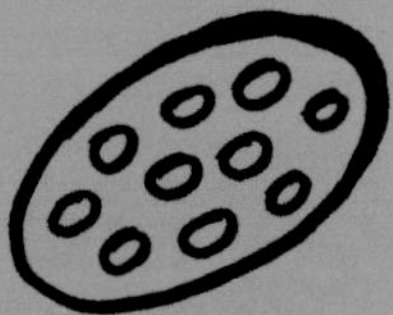

collecting turtle eggs

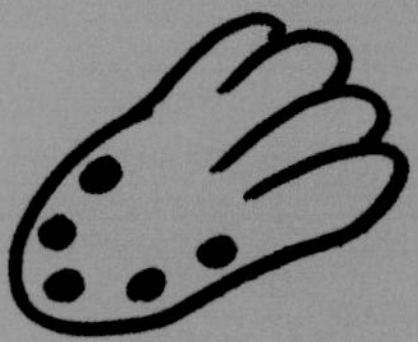

water mussel

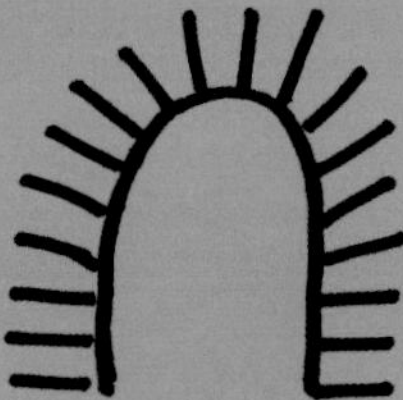

body painted
woman dancing

With regard to the above, we need to take note of the following:

1. The Emu is the earth and the Dreaming knowledge emanates from her along ancient pathways. Some tribes know this force as *kurunba*. In Britain these tracks are known as ley lines and in China they are dragon paths.

2. The 'white' element in initiation is related to a universal albino theme in the origins of a bringer of wisdom (see Revelation 1:14).

3. Empires decimate cultures and tourism generates greed. The above is a comprehensive collection of what has survived; but even so, in some cases the meaning is confused. The above rendition is my very best effort based on my knowledge and experience. There can be little or no doubt that the original Australian system was once very sophisticated.

Part Two
Some Dreamtime Stories

Two Sisters

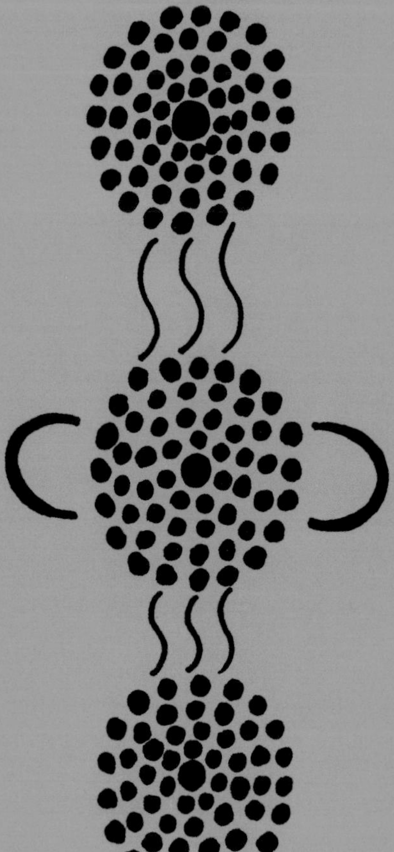

There is a constellation of three stars that were once known as *Three* Sisters (very probably the three stars of Orion's belt). In the beginning, the three very beautiful young women who occupied each of these stars decided to come down to earth and look around. While here, one met two men—always depicted as snakes—and fell in love with them. Because she had had contact with mortals, she was no longer allowed to return to the star world. Therefore, only two went back, and now that constellation is known as *Two* Sisters. She, who remained, then took the form of Emu. As a bird that cannot fly, she is symbolically a prisoner on earth. But her role becomes that of the Earth Mother, married to and at sometime estranged from Father Sky.

The Greeks spoke of three fates called Moirai (Marys) and the Egyptians had, as previously mentioned, a Goddess with three heads.

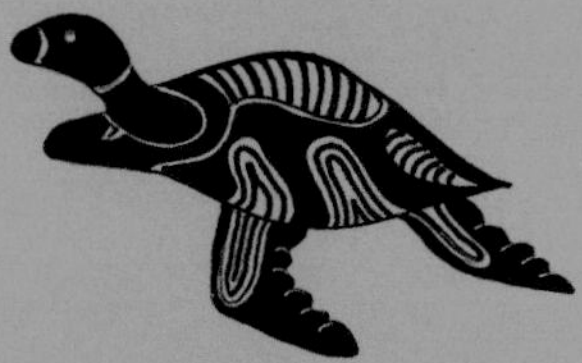

The Tnatanja Pole

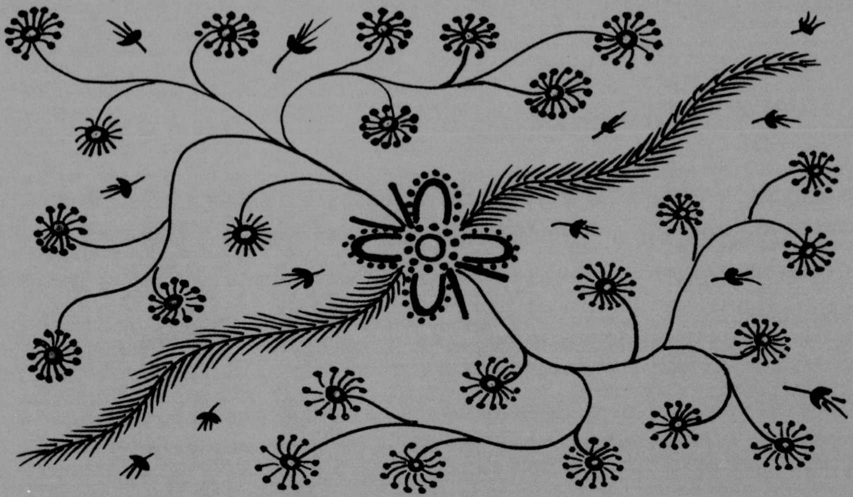

The Tnatanja Pole seen from above, with men and women seated in a circle around Emu and learning the Dreaming knowledge after their creation.

Emu had a very long pole whose base was in the bowels of the earth and whose top reached up to heaven. It grew branches that stretched up to the stars and it regularly sprouted emu feathers. She made her home atop this pole so that she would always be able to see her star of origin. Every now and again, the wind would blow some of the feathers from the pole. Those that fell to the left became women and those that fell to the right became men. That's how people were made in the Churinga (Dreamtime).

Some form of tree of knowledge, holy mountain or temple of creation (wisdom being the seed of Father Sky), is found in pretty well every culture on earth. The subsequent multiplicities of Adams and Eves are clearly references to the left and right hemispheres of the brain, the one and the zero. The Greek philosopher Plato terms these 'the same and the other'. Basically, the ancient view was that 'all' is mind; the two hemispheres of the brain (internal and external) are seen as generating the two physical genders.

Turtle and Emu

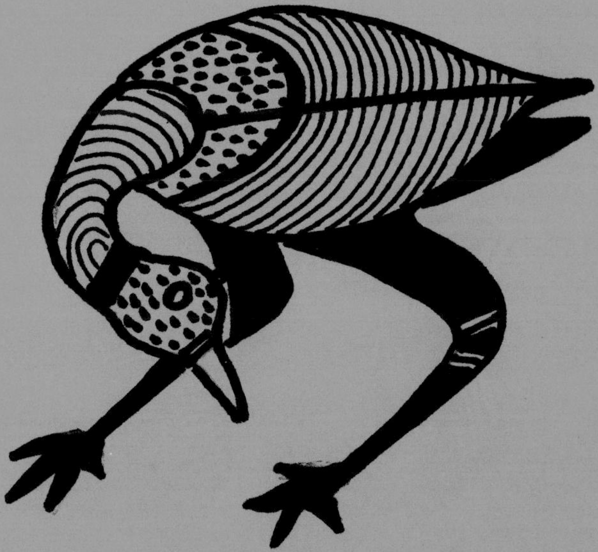

Turtle and Emu simply couldn't get on together. It was not that one was good and the other bad; it was a clash of personalities. When the people went to war, Emu did not want to see her children fighting, so she went into hiding. To make sure her offspring could always find her, she drew a map of her hiding place on Turtle's back, so that her children would see it easily and Turtle could not see it at all. Western tradition says that Scorpio (Turtle) was a contender for the thirteenth (lunar) sign of the zodiac. But ultimately, the true claimant was the moon goddess (Emu in Australia)—hence the mutual animosity.

The Path of the Emu

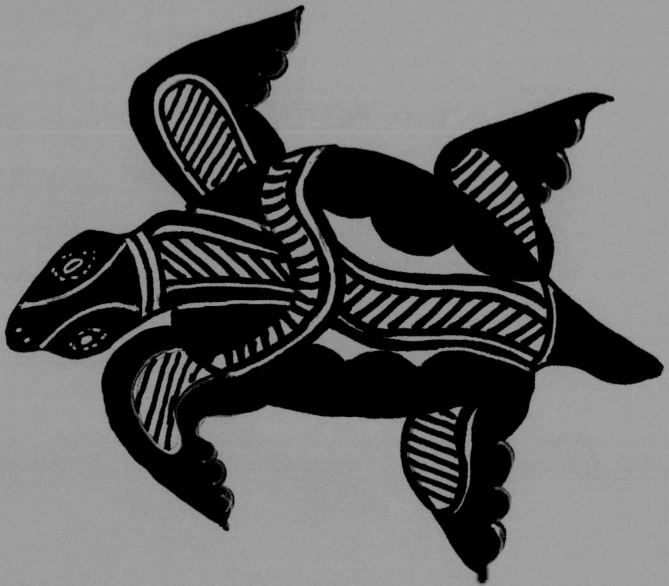

The map on the Turtle's back was called the Path of the Emu. The witchetty grubs and honey ants knew it well, for it was they who trod it regularly so that they might feed and sustain her.

The Greek Goddess hid in a labyrinth and was guarded by a Minotaur (a Gemini - o - Taurus).

As previously mentioned, ancient myths are concerned with two astronomical factors: the precession of the equinoxes and the measurement of time. The latter may be divided into either twelve (solar) or thirteen (lunar) segments. Invariably, there is always an interloper wanting to take the place of the lost thirteenth tribe of heavenly wanderers. In the Western zodiac, he is Scorpio, which the Aborigines call Turtle, as do the Japanese. In another publication, The Thirteenth Stone, *I have been able to show that the lost sign is Coma Berenices in Virgo—a copious head of hair.* *See* The Seven Sisters *on page 14.*

Another important point here is that in the West, the equivalent to the honey ants is the bee—particularly the queen bee with men as her drones.

Great Kangaroo

When the Great Flood came, it was left to Great Kangaroo to organize the animal people to push back the waters. Afterwards, he spat out all the different tongues that the people of the earth (*tya*) would speak.

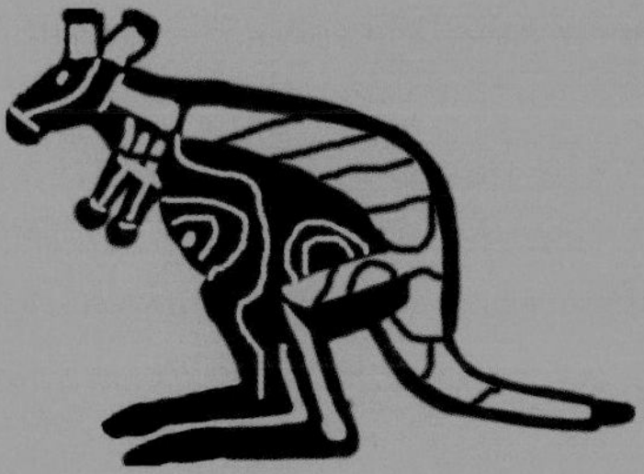

The Great Byamee

It was Byamee, a meek, mild-mannered man with incredible wisdom, who was sent to teach men a code of law. Some say his home was at the bottom of the sea and others speak of his origins being in the Milky Way (in Taurus).

In Sumer and Babylon, the hero Gilgamesh was born of a cow and in Egypt, Horus was born of Isis, a cow. In the Dead Sea Scrolls, the hero, a bringer of secret wisdom, is also a Taurean. But emergence from a chaotic watery abyss is also universal. The wise fisherman or part fish, part man (the Oannes—the root word for Jonathan) is found in Britain (as Merlin), in Scripture (as Elijah) and in South America, Japan and beyond.

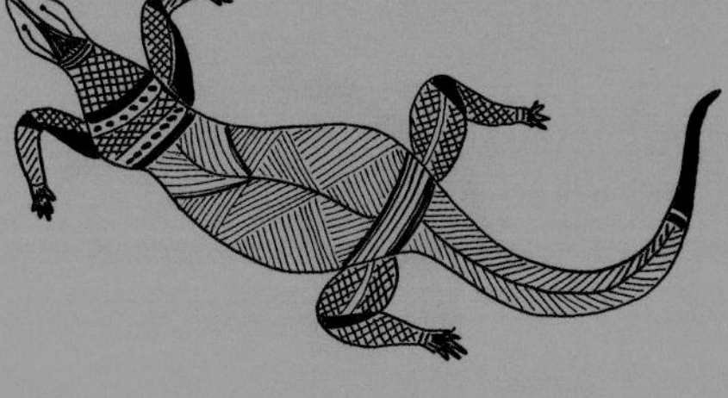

The Flying Grinding Stones

It was at the first ever Corroboree (a festive and/or sacred meeting) that Byamee encountered the two women who had lost their grinding stones. After an all-out search of the camp, Byamee spotted two Wunda spirits carrying them away above the trees. He reached out his hand and turned some of the women into brown pigeons and they chased the Wundas till they tired and dropped the stones. Where they fell, there sprang up a great mountain of grinding stones.

Stones fall from heaven as meteorites and may thus be used as symbols for stars. The ancient cosmic temple or Star City was where men said they could speak to the gods, or pass through it and walk around heaven. Their method, they said, was to utter the unspeakable name for which 'Jehovah' was an abbreviation. This has always been politely translated as 'I am that I am'; it actually means 'mind your own business'. Later, when the Goddess was lost or went into hiding, men built the temple with only twelve stones; she was the stone the builders rejected.

The First Didjeridu

It is said the first didjeridu was made by a shaman by cutting off his penis. This is why women are forbidden to play it.

The fact is that for those of us who look beyond the didgeridoo as a purely musical instrument or piece of unique artwork, there is a strong possibility of developing a *mytholodia* in which, through music, we may bring together as one both the spirit of the past and the new world. This, in my opinion, is the fundamental contribution which Aboriginal Australia is quietly waiting to gift to the world. Perhaps the central significance of the didgeridoo, as we shall see, is that it not only has a phallic appearance, it is said to be the voice of the long lost mythical Rainbow Snake called *Yurlunggur*, who's vibrations created the physical world. As with so many other cultures, the snake is a symbol of wisdom in Aboriginal Australia.

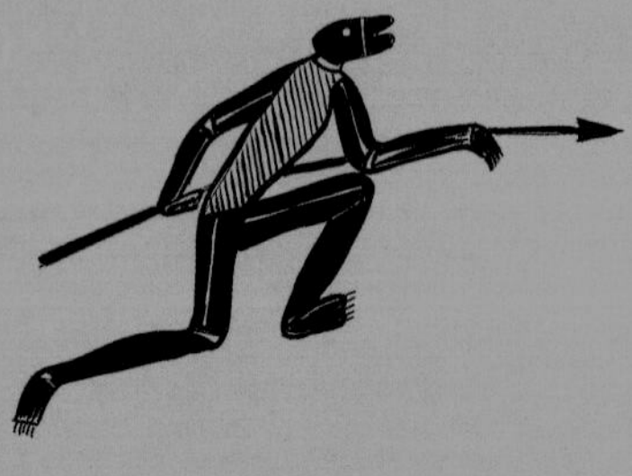

Byamee and the Bullroarer

The voice of Byamee was said to repose in the bullroarer, which was fashioned by the All-Father from a rejected stone. This has recently been made famous by Crocodile Dundee, as the 'bush telegraph' he spun above his head. Because of its sacredness, it was forbidden to the sight of women and the uninitiated.

Rainbow Serpent

This mythic creature has two genders. As the creator of the rainbow, he is the masculine sun. As an excavator of river beds and dweller in waterholes and lagoons, she is the feminine Earth-Spirit.

The Seven Sisters

These were water girls who had had a curse inflicted upon them, thus their only friends were crocodiles, fish and leeches, but they craved human companionship. Living in water, they had developed a smooth and slippery skin and so no one was able to catch them, no matter how they tried. One day a hunter saw one of the women just below the surface with her long hair floating to the top. He dived, grabbed her hair, wound it around his arm and brought her to shore. He then lit a fire and held her over the smoke to take away her curse. They married and lived happily together. Their renown as hunters subsequently spread far and wide, even to her mother and father who lived high up in a banyan tree.

The connection here with the Greek Rainy Hyades (of which one was lost) in Taurus, making this particular sister the star Alcyone in the Pleiades, is irrefutable. Her captor passing her through the smoke to remove the curse establishes him as being the sun (Father Sky). And then there is the symbolism of the tree which, as a tree of knowledge, is another symbol for the temple of stones or Star City.

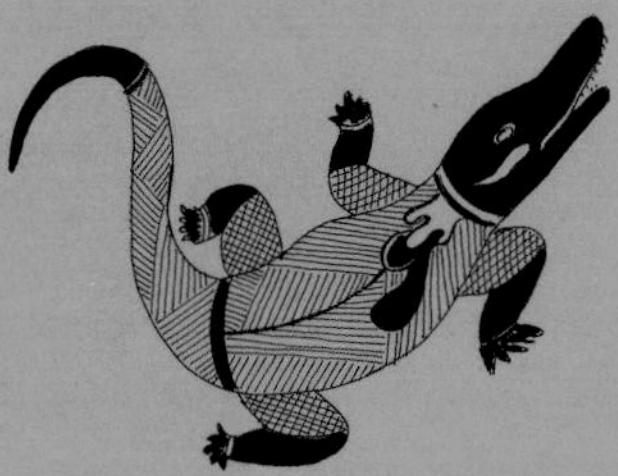

Byamee and Yhi

Byamee is probably the kindest and most considerate of all creators. He begins as a non-corporeal being. Yhi was a feminine counterpart to him and was the goddess of the sun. It was she who gave light, warmth and life to what Byamee created. But, for man, there was yet another ingredient required—intelligence, the essence of soul life. And this could only come from the All-Father in the form of a new creation.

In this process, as Byamee took on sinew and flesh, the world sank into turmoil; flood and darkness were upon the face of the earth. When Byamee finally manifested as a man, to his great surprise and disappointment, few if any of the animal people recognised him.

Byamee first formed man from the dust of the earth but, seeing his loneliness, made woman from a yacca tree, and then returned to his home in the Milky Way.

Not only in this tale, but in the entire corpus of Byamee material, it is hard to ignore the parallels with the New Testament epic. We need also to consider here the Sumerian Nin Kharsag. But ultimately, even with the limitations of a book of this size, it is obvious that the Aborigines were once party to a universal system.

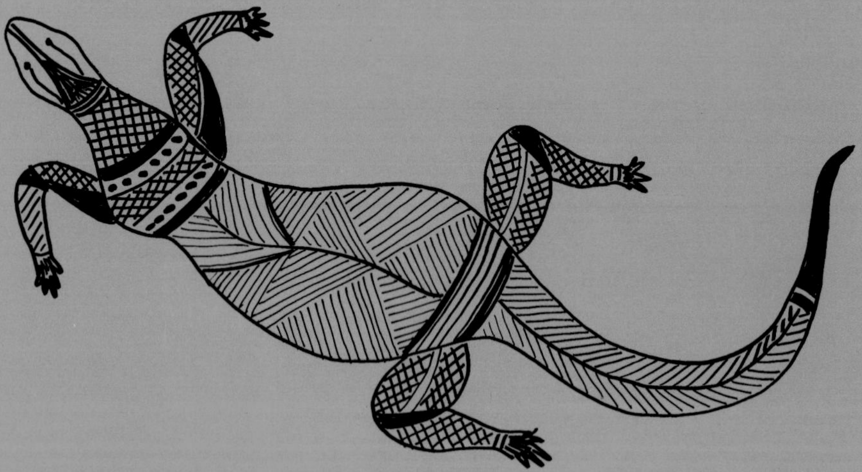

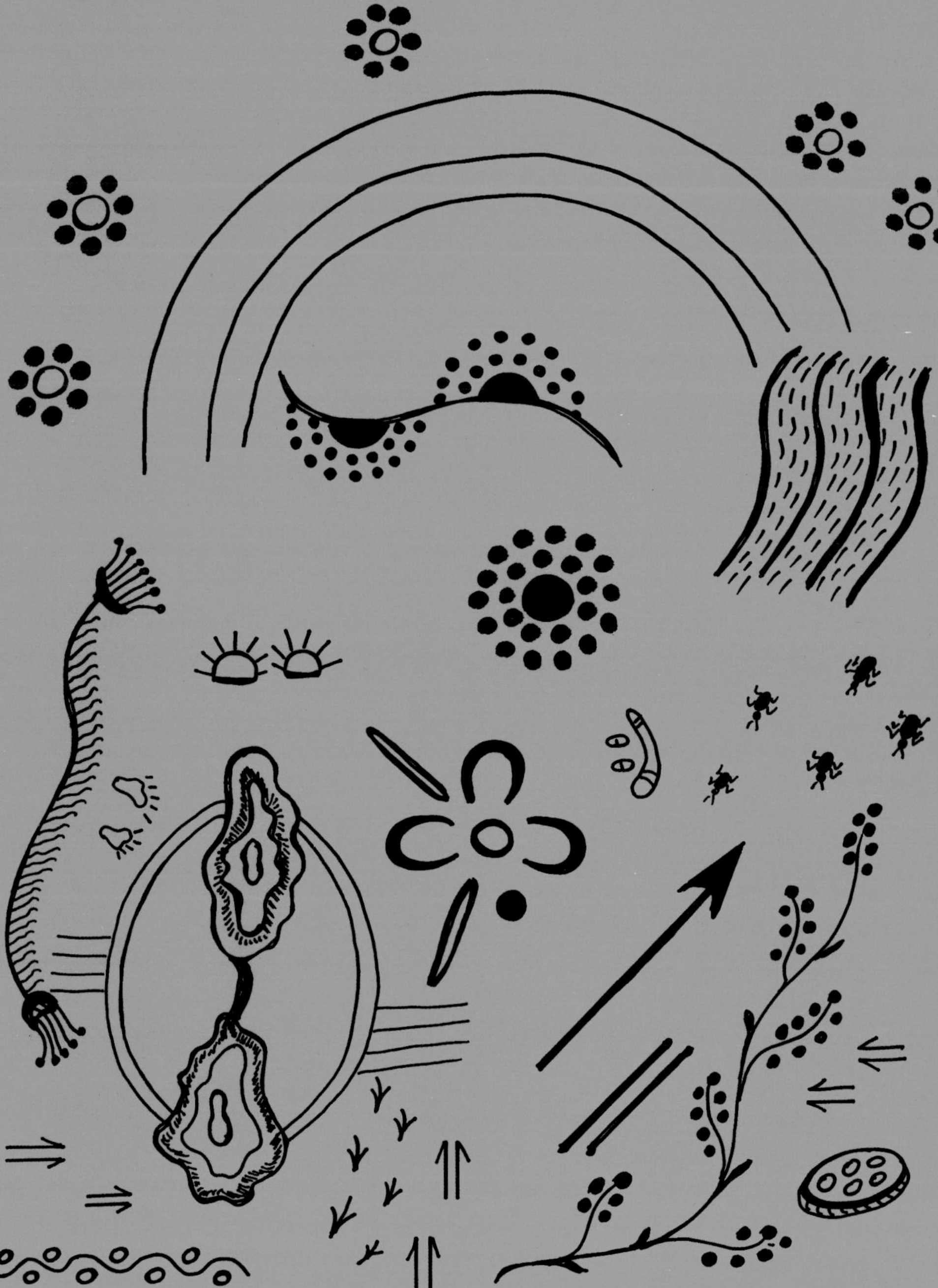

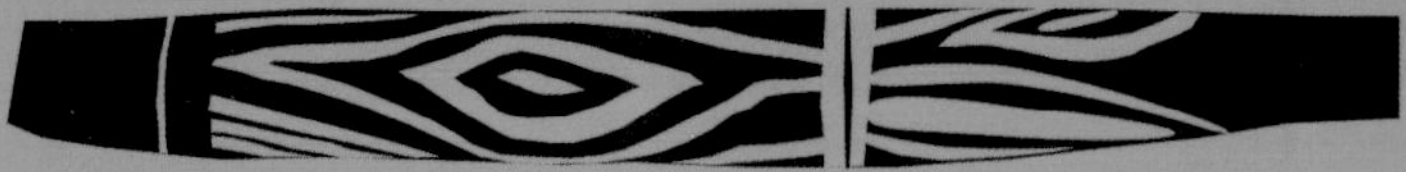

Aboriginal Art is a vast and complex subject filled with many mutually contradicting opinions. It needs to be said that this small book cannot and does not take any of these into account. Indeed it is specifically a 'Beginner's Guide' with no pretensions to anything more.

So, if you are a visitor to Australia, seat yourself beneath your hotel's air-conditioning or by the pool and read. Then amble down to your local art gallery and amaze yourself at the ease with which, unaided, you can now read the stories in the paintings.

If you are an educator teaching Aboriginal Studies, it is proposed that you go through this book with your class and then encourage them to paint or draw their own Dreamtime stories.

For many years, while working in my Fremantle gallery, I was constantly asked, 'What do these symbols mean?' Each time this happened, I thought to myself, 'Why isn't there a little book that would unpretentiously answer that question? It's about time', I considered, 'that they *did something about it.' Realising that this is probably the most common sin on earth, I admitted to being one of 'them' and got on with it. This little book has since amazed me how easily and simply it unravels the great mystery of the meaning of Aboriginal art. Enjoy!*

R Lewis

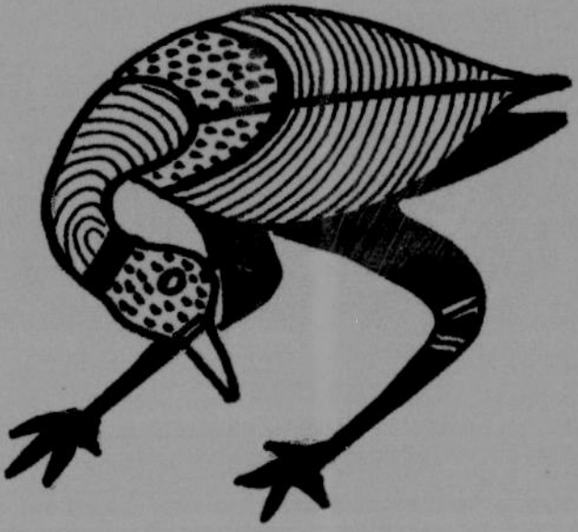

9 780646 403687